Has Anyone Seen My Mom?

A Guide to Never Letting Go!

This book is dedicated to my mom,
Jean Marie Ivey Timlick,
born Sept 14, 1930–Oct 21, 2015.

Copyright © 2023 Craig Timlick

All rights reserved. No part of this book may be reproduced or used in any manner without the prior written permission of the copyright owner, except for the use of brief quotations in a book review.

To request permissions, contact the publisher at: publisher@villagebooks.com

ISBN: 9798218192181
LOC: 2023906740

Cover art by Owen Paznokas
Layout by Owen Paznokas
Printed in the USA by Village Books.

Village Books
1200 11th St
Bellingham WA,
98225
Villagebooks.com

To my sisters, Jodi and Bev, my daughter Sarah, and my wife Kelly

Table of Contents

Introduction
Chapter 1: The Journey Begins
Chapter 2: The First Moment of Grief
Chapter 3: The Signs
Chapter 4: Transitioning to Assisted Living
Chapter 5: Denial
Chapter 6: Roller Coaster of Emotions
Chapter 7: Family Stress
Chapter 8: Learning to Laugh and Cry Together
Chapter 9: Becoming Aware of Her Pain
Chapter 10: It Is Just Time To Say Goodbye
Epilogue: The Reality of Today
Tribute
About the Author

....6
....8
....13
....18
....24
....30
....33
....38
....46
....52
....55
....59
....61
....62

Introduction

Ask not what is in front of you but believe in the memories of the past as they can reconnect you to someone you love.

You can't change the past, but it can shape the future, even given the challenges of whatever illness has entered a person's life!

~Anonymous

When I was six years old, my mom took me to Kmart to buy a new bike. I was so excited, I couldn't wait. We entered the store hand in hand, I was so taken aback by all of the amazing things (I loved sports, and I could not get enough of the sporting goods department in the store). My attention, of course, was on everything except my mom. I walked away from her just amazed at the hockey gloves, sticks, baseball gloves, bikes, etc. I could barely speak. Suddenly I realized I was alone and had wandered away on my own. My mom was nowhere to be found. The panic set in!!! I started running throughout the store asking everyone:

<u>"Has anyone seen my mom?"</u>

I eventually found her in another part of the store. I was so overcome with emotions; I could not stop crying and did not dare let go of her hand, squeezing it hard, never wanting to feel that sense of panic ever again.

As you fast-forward, when my mom was struggling with Alzheimer's/dementia, I felt that same panic of running through the store as a six-year-old, unable to find or reach my mother. I thought I would never have that same feeling again as I sat in front of her while she struggled to even know who I was.

This book is a simple story of a son that drifted away from his family in life but found himself coming back to be beside his mother in challenging times, fighting to reconnect and be supportive. In my heart of hearts, I hope you enjoy what I have written and that you learn that it is possible to reconnect with someone you love, even though health barriers say you can't.

Chapter 1
The Journey Begins

I find myself writing this book at age fifty-seven; this journey started approximately ten years ago when I was forty-seven. I was living in Toronto with my wife and daughter, enjoying life. I had a successful career, was active in sports and leading a healthy lifestyle—basically life was good! I had moved several times for my career, starting in Vancouver, British Columbia, where I grew up and finally coming to live in Burlington, Ontario, near Toronto.

I had been very blessed in life, attending university doing my BA as well as MBA with thoughts of completing a PhD or doctorate, but unfortunately, I never got that far after finding out how sick my mom really was. Funny how your life priorities change and certain things get placed on the shelf or on hold due to changes in your life.

My first year of university, living in my bachelor's apartment.

Unfortunately, I had drifted away from any connection with my family as they were on the West Coast and we on the East. I am not going to mislead you here: there was some bitterness from my family as I had married into a very strong, involved Italian family that was very supportive of both Sophia, my wife at the time, and myself. The hard part was my family just seemed to be on the outside looking in. We talked on the phone from time to time and had quick visits here and there during vacations if we were in Vancouver, but the true sense of connecting seemed to have been lost. My mom did visit with us twice, once when we lived in Winnipeg and another time when we lived in Toronto. Funny thing was it seemed like we were strangers and struggled just to have a conversation. At the end of her visit, on the way to the airport in Toronto, she had a meltdown and told me I never lived up to my family commitments and didn't support her and my sisters.

After a few months passed by, we managed to resolve the issue; I think it was important for her to make a point with me not to focus on just my married family as I had an immediate family that loved me and was proud of me as well.

Time passed and we went back to having the weekly phone calls of "Hi, how are you?" with a quick update. We did this for several years but never seemed to reestablish our connection, though we both tried.

I looked forward to the weekly call with her, but there was one call she made to me that changed me forever. It was a Sunday, and I was working in my home office. The phone rang, and it was my mom, who was extremely upset, telling me that my oldest sister, Ollie, was in the hospital for what they thought was just minor issues as she had been struggling to get healthy. They had found a tumor on her bladder and after a biopsy determined it was cancer. Over the next year, she had the normal battery of cancer-related treatments, which all took their toll on her, both physically and mentally. Throughout this entire time, I was in a stage of denial, believing that Ollie would always get through this!

My mom at the beach just trying to coupe

It's funny how denial can be the crutch that you lean on in difficult times, but reality always sets in sooner or later. I talked with Ollie over the phone, trying my best to see her when I was in Vancouver, which included several visits to the hospital.

Ollie's illness would be a watershed moment in all our lives that sent the entire family in different stages of grief, but for my mom it was down a road of depression, dementia, and Alzheimer's, a road that would take her further and further away from all of us.

Chapter 2
The First Moment of Grief

*"Do not weep any longer, for I will reward you,"
says the Lord.*
~Jeremiah 31:16 NLT

After my sister was told she was cancer free, I could see a real change in my mom; she seemed so relieved. Unfortunately, that did not last long as the emotional storm was about to begin.

I received a call from my mom that Ollie had been over for a visit at her house and was concerned that her back was hurting. My mom was a retired head nurse with thirty-five years of experience. After looking at Ollie's back, Mom called an ambulance and she was taken to Surrey Memorial Hospital. After seeing a doctor, she was then taken to Vancouver General Hospital and placed in the palliative care center, where she was told that she had limited time to live.

My mom called me to tell me the bad news, and I have to be honest, my first reaction was that this could not be happening. I spoke with Ollie on the phone, and she was of course very confused and emotionally lost, to say the least. She had just been told that her cancer had returned and was incurable and she would have to enter a hospice care unit. How does one even comprehend the sheer magnitude of how this would impact her husband and four children? Ollie's battle with cancer came to an end on June 3, 2006.

After Ollie passed, I was still in shock and caught up in my own grief, not knowing which way to turn. I kept telling myself, *This cannot be happening!*

I attended Ollie's celebration of life and spoke on her behalf. I tried to capture what I thought my sister's purpose in life was. I realize God determines that, but I truly felt her purpose was, in my opinion, being a great mom to her kids. In my speech, I described what I thought was the definition of a great mom and tried to offer comfort to her children.

"A great mom is a person who has that sixth sense, who is able to always know when and where to be. She shows up for you unexpectedly just knowing that she is needed. A great mom knows what to say to make your day better, and

Saying goodbye and celebrating the life of my sister. This was the last picture taken of my mom and my sister Ollie together.

she knows what to say to bring you up in those days that feel really low when nothing seems to be working. A great mom is a person who is loving and caring in all moments in life. She knows how to communicate in such a way that her life coaching gets you back on track but also gives you a sense of comfort. A great mom is someone you know is always around for you no matter what!

"The key is that, no matter where she is, your mother will always be alive in your heart and mind. Although your mom has passed away and left this world, all you need to do is go to that place in your heart, and she will continue to be there for you."

As I was giving this speech, what I will never forget is the look in my mom's eyes, staring into space as I spoke from the podium. She seemed lost and defeated. I was sure that look would pass, but to my shock, it never did, as her health dramatically changed after this.

Once I returned to Toronto, nothing seemed important. My career, family . . . I found myself very alone, struggling to make sense of everything. Memories popped up in my head at various times of day of Ollie when we were kids, things that I had not thought of in years. I tried seeing a counselor (her name was Barb) to help me understand why I was struggling. The guilt that I was placing on myself was extremely high; however, once you dug down to the root issue, I felt guilty because I never had the opportunity to say goodbye. Barb suggested that I write a letter and go to the cemetery and read it to Ollie.

I agreed and did just that. As I read my letter out loud to Ollie, it allowed me to share what was on my heart and the deep loss that I was feeling. I needed her to know what an amazing sister she was and the impact she had on me growing up. I am not sure, but I had a warm feeling and presence of God at that moment.

    Unfortunately, the stress I felt was taking its toll on my marriage of twenty-five years, and a few years after Ollie's death, Sophia and I ended our marriage. She said that she just did not know how to help me or be part of what I was going through. I wish that I could have been more open and shared with her what it was, but I did not know how to express it or who to turn to. Grief is a funny thing, and it places a tremendous amount of stress on you as a person. You feel lost in life as you have known it, and nothing seems that important anymore.

Chapter 3
The Signs

For I can do everything through Christ, who gives me strength.

~Philippians 4:13 NLT

After my sister Ollie died, my mom became very distant. I returned home after Ollie's funeral services and did my best to reach out to Mom over the phone just to check in with her, and I did my best to see her when I was in Vancouver for business. Living in Toronto at the time made it very difficult to see her as much as I wanted.

Unfortunately, I was having my own issues at the time, just trying to come to grips with the loss of my sister. I always thought she would get through this very difficult health challenge.

When I was in Vancouver for business, I found myself stopping by her grave just to talk. I still believe that she could hear me. It has taken me a long time to feel okay with her loss, though

I'm not sure if I will ever feel totally at peace. Time will tell.

My mom seemed to be changing through this entire process. When I would call her on the phone, she started to ask me really strange questions about my dad. The reason I found that strange was because he had died almost twenty-five years before.

The calm before the storm . . . dementia.

The strangest call I got was while I was on a business trip in the US. In the middle of the night, I got a call on my cell phone from my mother, and when I answered, she started telling me to hurry up and get home as I had curfew at 10:00 p.m., and it was significantly past that. I tried to explain to her that I was forty-seven years old at the time, but that just made her very angry, and she told me that I did not know what I was talking about. I called my sister Jodi the next day, and she told me that Mom was acting very strange and seemed very depressed and had given up on life after losing Ollie.

I decided to take a trip out to Vancouver and check in on her myself. I arrived at her home on a very rainy Vancouver day. I walked up the stairs and knocked on the door, but no answer. So I walked in and called out, "Mom, it's me, Craig."

I found her sitting in her chair, looking out the window with a blank stare on her face.

"Mom, what are you doing?"

Her expression didn't change. "Just watching the rain. And thinking about life and Ollie."

I noticed that she was not eating very well and had lost a lot of weight. I picked up the phone and called Jodi again, and after a long discussion, Jodi asked me to go with her and Mom to the doctor. We set a date and time with the doctor, and I stayed a few extra days on this trip to ensure I could attend.

Mom was very angry at having to go, and you

could see it in her face. When we arrived at the doctor's office, we all headed into a small exam room where the doctor asked my mom how she was, and of course she said that she was fine, no issues. He decided to test Mom by giving her a number of things to remember, and to my surprise, she responded very well. She almost acted a little smug and grinned at me with an "I told you so" attitude.

He then pointed at my sister Jodi and asked her who she was. She responded correctly that it was her daughter Jodi. Then the doctor turned to me and asked her who I was; shockingly, she responded that I was her brother Keith! I have to say, I was a little overwhelmed. She tried to correct herself, saying I simply looked like Keith. My uncle was seventy years old with a doctorate of medical engineering. No offense to my uncle, but I did not think that I looked like a seventy-year-old man—at least in my opinion!!

That was just the start of what was to come.

Mom started going over to the neighbors' and asking if this was 1125 Kendale View, my parents' old address in North Delta, where we grew up. At that point, we needed to decide to get her some counseling, but once again Mom said no, as there was nothing wrong with her. We attempted to take her for a visit to a new assisted living home, just to see how she would like it. That turned into a battle just getting her there. The funny thing was we had a very nice tour of the facility, and we sat down with the administrator so that Mom could answer a few questions. She sat there holding her handbag with a very angry look on her face.

The administrator began, "So Mrs. Timlick, why have you chosen our facility?"

Mom responded in a direct voice, "She made me come here," and pointed at my sister Jodi. Unfortunately, my mom's older sister Margaret was already in a home, and she told Mom that once you go in, you only come out on a stretcher, which made things even worse!

My mother always had a very dry sense of humor, but I could tell this time she was not kidding and seemed very upset with both Jodi and myself for even bringing her to this place. Both Jodi and Bev, my other sister who lives in Calgary, and I talked about it after and agreed that there was little that we could do but wait and see if she would change or snap out of it. Unfortunately, that was not to be.

I returned back to Toronto to work and family, but the calls continued with even stranger requests, and I was at a loss for what to do.

With all the strange behavior, my sisters Jodi and Bev took the lead and finally got Mom to move into an assisted living home in the Newton area of Surrey, BC.

Chapter 4
Transitioning to Assisted Living

By the time I got out to visit her, Mom had only lived in that facility for approximately two months. She had a nice suite with a kitchen, and all of the local residents seems very friendly as they would all knock on Mom's door to head down to dinner in the main hall together.

I was back in town once again on business, so I took the time to visit Mom one evening. Wow, what a great place! And security was tight; I kept thinking that I could break out of a federal prison easier than this place, but it gave me a feeling that she would be safe, no matter what. I finally arrived at her room, and we sat and talked for hours. However, the strangest thing happened then that I would never forget.

During our conversation, the look on her face changed, and she wanted to know if Ollie knew that she had moved, and she was very worried about it. Given that Ollie had passed away two years before, I tried to talk around the topic and then finally decided to just tell the truth.

"Mom, Ollie died from cancer two years ago."

Boy, what a mistake. She became so upset, and I had a hard time getting her to settle down. I should have followed the golden rule of being with an Alzheimer's patient: "Whatever they tell you, just go with it."

Mom's stay at this home was short as she managed to do the unexpected!

"The Great Escape"

Late one night, Mom stayed up worrying about Ollie, and she put her coat on and managed to get the sliding glass door open in her unit. An alarm was supposed to go off, but unfortunately it did not. This was approximately 4:00 a.m., and, walker in hand to support her, she headed out and down the street to King George Boulevard, which used to be a highway.

It was a terrible night, pouring rain, but she was on a mission. I think she got about ten blocks before she fell forward, landing on her side. She was not able to get up, but none of the passing cars would stop and help as they either thought she was just some homeless person or were too busy to help.

Finally, a man stopped his car and called 911 for help. I don't know this man, but I will always be grateful for his help. I sometimes think of him as a gift from God as he certainly saved her that night.

Surrey Memorial Hospital

Mom ended up at Surrey Memorial Hospital, where she had nursed for thirty-five years. She was placed in a lockdown ward, and the next challenge for her was getting over pneumonia after being caught lying in the rain on the street.

I was still living in Toronto at the time and took a flight out to Vancouver to see Mom at the hospital. When I arrived, I could not get over how much she had changed again in just a few short weeks. She was in a shared room but was very weak. I was back and forth to see her just to hold her hand and provide some level of comfort several times, but the good news was that she responded well to the treatments and, on my third visit, had really bounced back.

The nurses on the floor that cared for her were amazing. After realizing my mom was a former head nurse at that hospital for over thirty-five years and knowing how good she was at her job, they found ways to include her as an honoree in the staff meetings. It made me proud of the person she was. Mom must have felt like she was back in time! They would invite her down to the nurses' meeting and give her a clipboard and ask her what she thought. This simple act of helping her reconnect to her past was amazing; I had never seen my mom so happy. I visited her one evening, and there she was in the nurses' station helping out, at least so she thought. Seeing her like that confirmed just how many people she had helped in her career.

I can't tell you how many people I went to school with came up to me at a high school reunion that I attended years later and told me that my mom was amazing and had delivered all of their kids as the head nurse at Surrey Memorial Hospital. This point of connection gave me a true picture of how special she really was and how many people she had touched and helped in her role as head nurse. I wondered what I had missed earlier in life by not being close to her.

Mom giving me a small birthday cake in celebration of my birth on July 1, also Canada Day! Mom always told me the fireworks were for me, but I didn't believe her.

I've always found my mom to have a great sense of humor. I decided on this visit to get her up and walking around the halls of the floor that she was on. She had a walker, so doing this was slow going for sure. We had walked around the floor three times, and we had to pass this group of old men sitting in wheelchairs. The third time that we walked by, one of the senior men reached out to slap my mother on the ass. To say the least, I was a little shocked! I turned to my mom and said, "Did that man just slap you on the ass?"

She responded in a very upbeat voice, "Yes! Let's go around again!!!!"

This was a moment of connection—although not what a son wants to see or hear about from his mom. When I grew up, sex and emotions were never talked about. But this was a clear moment with my mom where I got to see her and connect with her through humor.

The funny thing about being in a hospital, you would think that you are there to get better for whatever sickness or issue you have, but during her stay, Mom managed to get a bacterial infection in her intestines, and we were not sure if she was going to make it. But thankfully, after several months of this, Mom was able to recover to the point that Jodi could then work with social services to find her a placement in a home that could provide the care and support she needed.

Chapter 5
Denial

Please forgive me, Father, for allowing fear and worry to dominate my thoughts. I am your child, and I know that your power working in me is greater than what anyone or anything can do to me or against me.

Joel Osteen, Daily Readings from Your Best Life Now

Three months at Surrey Memorial Hospital was a lot, but I kept telling myself that she would eventually snap out of it. Each time I visited Mom, she seemed to be developing new issues. I think I was up to see her at least a dozen times or so, and each time, I noticed some change in her, both physically and mentally. She was challenged with new issues every week from a physical standpoint, getting sick several times. Though it was more the mental changes that were most noticeable. She would talk about things from her past, mostly her childhood, like they happened yesterday. She was very fixated on her parents and why they had not come up to see her. Several times, she would talk to me as if I were her brother, Keith.

One day, when I arrived in the lobby of the home she was in, she asked me if I had seen my father, who had been dead for twenty years. Remembering that golden rule of just going with whatever an Alzheimer's patient says, I said yes.

"How did he look?" she asked.

"Really good," I said.

She replied, "You know, Craig, your dad always looked good..."

We both laughed.

I spent a tremendous amount of time visiting my mom, yet each time, I kept telling myself this couldn't be happening. I became very overwhelmed every time I visited her; she was changing rapidly, and it was never for the good. The changes were not only in her thoughts and memory but also in her physical appearance. When Mom came into the care home, she was walking with a walker. About a year later, she was in a wheelchair and movement was extremely difficult.

Each person in our family reacted differently to Mom's worsening condition. My sister Jodi was Mom's main caregiver and tended to be her loving protector—her nurse's training, I guess. My other sister Bev tended to react in loving preparation, thinking she needed to focus on getting ready for the day that Mom's life would come to an end. As for me, I had a constant feeling of contradicting fears—not wanting her life to end, but at the same time not wanting her to suffer. Who knows which of us was right or wrong; I just kept praying for Mom, asking God to welcome her as gently as possible.

 I don't think anyone is ever truly ready for the passing of a loved one, and a state of denial is a way of coping. With time, I realized the comfort, peace, and hope that God's word brought to me. I trusted that God placed us in this world to do his work. This trust allowed me to accept the situation a little bit more and be grateful for the life Mom had lived up until that point.

Chapter 6
Roller Coaster of Emotions

The faithful love of the Lord never ends! His mercies never cease. Great is his faithfulness; his mercies begin afresh each morning.
Lamentations 3:22-23 NLT

During this time, all of us focused on caring for our mom. I was still living in Toronto, and I can recall getting several calls from my sister regarding having to take mom to the hospital, and each time I felt a sense of panic. I then made the decision to relocate back to Vancouver to be closer to my mom and be able to help care for her. I felt this was a pivotal moment in my life and needed to do something to be of more support to my family.

Living in Vancouver allowed me to be present as these challenges came up. Late one Friday night, my sister Jodi called me to tell me Mom was sick with a bad cold, and they wanted to take her to the hospital. I drove over immediately, and when I arrived at the hospital, I had a feeling of being helpless as we waited for the doctor.

After waiting what seemed like hours, he finally came out to the waiting room and explained there was nothing they could do for Mom. I just kept praying for her and hoping that she would not be in any pain. We were on the phone a lot with my sister Bev, who still lived in Calgary, giving her updates as it was hard for her to be back and forth not knowing what and when things would change for the worse.

My sisters and I were doing our best to reconnect and provide each other with unconditional support. It wasn't easy, but we all tried. We all had other responsibilities and lived across the country. I love my sisters, and I know I could have been a better brother to them during this very challenging time, as the true focus was just on my mom. I take responsibility for my actions, but it's all too easy to become overwhelmed instead of reach out to your support network. Never forget there are people who are there to support you!

I always had a feeling of being alone, and it used to create a lot of panic in me. The feeling of panic was constant as I found myself caught on a roller coaster—from wondering if she was about to go, to thinking she was okay again. This constant flow of emotions overwhelmed me to the point that I was never sure what to think or what to do!

One summer evening, I was sitting alone in my home, after having relocated back to Vancouver. I decided to drop in and see how Mom was doing. Once I got to the floor, I found her and a group of residents sitting around the big flat-screen in the main hall. I walked in and, in a very upbeat voice, said, "So what are we doing?"

Each resident, including Mom looked at me as if I had lost my mind. I turned on the TV and, given it was Friday night, a CFL—Canadian Football League—game was on; I think it was Winnipeg versus Toronto.

I said to the group, "Okay, this side of the room is cheering for Winnipeg, and this side for Toronto." My mom started to get up, and I said, "Where are you going?"

She replied, "I need to move. I can't cheer for Toronto!"

I laughed. Once they were all seated, I got them doing the wave, and I have to say, I have never seen so many elderly people laughing and having fun. Even the nurses jumped in. These were the nights I felt like everything would be okay.

But then there were other times that plummeted me down. Another night, I showed up in the evening, and Mom had just had her bath—I swear the nurses used to hose them down; she looked like a drowned rat! She was sitting up in her chair, nicely dressed in her pajamas, and seemed very happy to see me. We began talking and everything was fine, but then she looked very confused all of a sudden. She asked me if I had seen Craig, and I responded that I was Craig. She started to scream at me that I was a stranger and demanded that I get out of her room—the bad language coming out of her mouth was shocking to say the least. The nurse came running down to her room and asked if I had an issue, and Mom responded she wanted this strange man out of her room. I decided it was best that I leave so that she would relax.

As soon as I got in my car, my iPhone started to ring; it was Mom.

"Thank goodness I reached you, Craig. I had some strange man in my room pretending to be you."

"Everything is fine, Mom. The nurse will help you and look out for any more strange men." I forced a laugh to assure her that all was well.

After hanging up, I started to cry in the

parking lot, realizing she was drifting away faster than I thought.

It's a funny thing with people suffering from Alzheimer's, they can struggle to remember people in the moment; however, they can recall past events from ten years ago like it was today. I had a doctor say to me once it was like a bomb exploded in my mom's brain, and she will use bits and pieces from her entire life to create reality. He said that the important thing was to never give up hope and to support her no matter what stage in Alzheimer's she is at.

I loved my mom so much even though we had our differences at times, like most families have. I had the constant desire to just say to her, "I love you! And it will be okay."

Chapter 7
Family Stress

Trust in the Lord with all your heart, and lean not on your own understanding; in all your ways acknowledge Him, and He shall direct your paths.

Proverbs 3:5-6 NLT

Mom came from a home where she had one sister and two brothers. My mom always had great family support but a lack of emotions. No one in her family ever said "I love you"! I asked her one day why she became a nurse, and she said her father told her that it was what she needed to do. Her other sisters and brother were also given the same direction but different professions. Mom had met my dad right after she graduated from nursing school. Those were the days student nurses lived at the hospital, and her parents had already rented her room, so even though my dad was her first real boyfriend, marriage followed quickly after they started dating.

Mom's graduation from nursing school.

Dad was a different story. He was raised in an orphanage, and he struggled with the concept of family. His mother had died giving birth to his youngest sister, Audrey. And after that, his own father took most of the kids to the Orange Home for Lost Children. I truly believe that my dad had a lifelong struggle with showing any sign or form of love and affection. It seemed to be all connected to the loss of his mother at a very young age and not having any support growing up as well, as the setting that he was in.

One thing was for sure, he left us all feeling no sense of connection to each other. Call it very simpleminded, but we all struggled to be a family and support each other. Our family home was always one where you never knew where you stood with my father, but my mom was the glue that tried her best to be supportive of each of us.

The last picture of my dad in his later life as well as one in his younger years.

I have mixed emotions looking at this picture as I was physically abused by my father, and it took me a long time to let go of what he did to me. He used to say that he was going to beat me within an inch of my life, and several times he came close. I am always amazed I survived those beatings. But I realize he had his own issues and suffered from alcoholism as well as prescription drug abuse. But my mom did her best to make this a home for all of us kids. My sisters have all said we would have been so much better off if Mom had left Dad, but she stood fast in trying to give us the best home possible.

This was our family home in North Delta.

I personally struggled being the only boy, and in my last year of high school, my mom and dad told me that they would work with me to get a job sweeping floors in a warehouse. I realized I needed to step away from both of them and work on myself as a person. Success in life is not measured by what you do or have but based on the person you are.

This placed a lot of pressure on me, but I realized I had to drive who and what I wanted to achieve in life. I am proud of the fact that I completed my BA and MBA and have been blessed to run several large companies in senior leadership roles as well as being associated with many great people. I have come to the belief that the emotional scars of the past can be healed and help you gain a better understanding of who you are and who you can be. So regardless of the situation you find yourself in, know that you can do this! If you give one hundred percent, you can get back one hundred percent . . . it all depends on you.

Family can be so hard on each other; I must be honest and say that I stepped away from my family after moving away and starting my career. I was struggling with our entire family dynamics. I felt like my family was not supportive of each other—they were more judgmental. Any interaction in my sisters' lives seemed to be more confrontational in whatever events my wife and

I attended, and it was just a matter of survival not to attend.

Living away from my family gave me a sense of peace and allowed me to focus on my own family and career at the time. My daughter, Sarah, who is now thirty, was off to university at the time on a sports program playing field hockey at the University of Toronto and winning a CIAU national championship and, of course, getting her degree. Today, she has a very successful career in the film industry in promotions and marketing. She has lived more in her current thirty years than I have in my whole life, from experiences, accomplishments, and career. She is my greatest accomplishment in life and never ceases to amaze me. I love you, Hun.

My wife and I had a great relationship up until Ollie's death; the hardest part after twenty-five years of marriage was our divorce. The funny thing was I had walked away from my own family because of all the issues and constant demands from them, as well as their negative approach to life and the effect it had on me. But after the divorce, I felt very much alone in life. The unfortunate part was I felt like I let my family down and did not support them.

When I went to counseling after Ollie's death,

the counselor told me I survived my childhood because I was able to focus on my sports, hockey and baseball, which allowed me to let go of the negative feelings that were placed on me. When my mom's brother came to visit her a few years into her stay in the care home, he said that he was proud of the man I had become. This stuck with me, given all the issues I faced from my father growing up and the limiting statements my mom would make concerning where my future would lead me.

As my marriage ended, I felt this overwhelming feeling that I needed to reconnect with Mom and my remaining sisters given the loss of Ollie and my mom becoming sick. However, that turned out to be more difficult than I thought; both of my remaining sisters were very much driven by control, and trying to reconnect turned into nothing more than a long-term debate over what should be done with Mom's care and what was good for the two of them.

Family stress is just an imbalance between demands facing a family and the ability of that family to handle the demands. In other words, if there are more stressful events happening to a family than the family can handle, family stress results. Family stress can be defined as any stressor that concerns one or more members of the family (or the whole system) at a defined time, which impacts the emotional connection between family members, their mood, well-being, and the maintenance of the family relationship.

In all this turmoil, I realized what was most important. What added value to my mother and to me was all the one-on-one time I spent with her, laughing, crying, and talking. That was the true value that I had regained by working through the family stress, and I would not give it up for anything.

Chapter 8
Learning To Laugh and Cry Together

Never be lazy, but work and serve the Lord enthusiastically.

Romans 12:11 NLT

My mom and I weren't always so distant. During my first year at university (1979–1982), Mom used to visit me with food. I had a small bachelor's suite in New Westminster, British Columbia, with rent of only $100 per month. It had a small cooking area and a foldout bed from the couch. My mom would occasionally stop by and bring me food as all the money I had was spent on paying for my university education. Kraft dinner and baked hot dogs with cheese was on the menu each night!

My mom and I in the kitchen taking a picture together—a moment that is forever in my heart!

We used to laugh a lot about my grocery shopping list at the local Woodward's Food Floor. They would have $1.49 Day Tuesday once a month and have both items (Kraft Dinner and hot dogs) on sale, and Mom used to say it was my stock up day!!

On my visits to the retirement home, I would reminisce with her about that time. "The life of a starving university student," I used to joke. I told her that it was a good thing she showed me how to cook those items, as I never would have gotten through university if she had not.

Over the years, Mom stopped walking and had to be moved around in a wheelchair. She never lost her sense of humor and always greeted you with a smile.

She was always ready to laugh, and as her illness progressed, laughter would connect us even deeper with each visit. One day I received a call from my sister that she needed help getting Mom to the dentist, and I told her I would take her. Funny, you always think things will be simple . . . I picked Mom up in the morning and took her out to my car by wheelchair. Getting her in the car was a challenge, given that I had bought a new Q60 Sport Coupe; I bet it took the better part of an hour just getting her into the front seat.

On the car ride to the dentist, a call came in through the speaker phone, and Mom had a great time talking out loud and laughing. She asked, "Can anyone really hear me?" She had seen cell phones before but not a hands-free device in a car.

We finally arrived at the dentist's office, and we were sitting in the lobby. My mother decided it was a good time to talk to me about my marriage and what happened. Sitting right in front of us was a young receptionist, maybe twenty-five years old at most. Once I explained that my marriage was over and I needed to move on, Mom decided to give me a sex talk. Given when I was sixteen, she handed me a pamphlet and told me not to get any girls in trouble and walked away, it was surprising she chose my late forties to reveal that I needed to put myself out there. In her words, "Craig, not having enough sex is not good for you."

Well, what should I say here? I could not bear to turn my head and look at the young lady at the desk, but when I did, she had a big smile on her face and said, "You need to listen to your mother," and laughed.

Whenever I visited Mom, I would do whatever I could to make her laugh. I would always tell her that the nurses called me because she was throwing too many parties. She would smile and say, "Not likely!" I would also say to her that I heard she was checking out the single men on the floor, and she would respond, "This floor doesn't have a lot of single men because I've already checked!"

On one of the best days I can remember, I told her that I knew I was her favorite son because she only had one. She laughed and told me, "Thank God for that." Then she went on to say that I had grown up to be the man that she had always wanted me to be, and she loved me very much! This was a big moment because she had never told me that growing up. Since she hadn't been raised that way, telling her kids she loved them was very difficult for her. But it was amazing she had finally told me, and it meant a lot.

I told her that night I was worried about her, and I was afraid that I would be away on business when she passed away. She took my hand with my eyes full of tears, and she said, "Craig, it is not about that moment in time. It is about all of the time we have spent together."

I felt like a huge burden was taken off me, and I could focus on being in the present with her and stop fearing what was eventually coming. My mother raised me in the United Church; she used to wake me up on Sunday mornings to take her to church, and I am grateful she did, as it gave me clear hope that being in this world is not forever and our home is with God.

Chapter 9
Becoming Aware of Her Pain

As Mom progressed with the disease, it became harder and harder to connect with her on every front. I found myself on a roller coaster of emotions—some days just trying to cope and others where I truly believed she would get better.

I tended to go to my sister's grave a lot just to talk with her and spend some quality time, even though she had passed away. It had been eight years since my sister passed away, but the pain seemed like it just started yesterday. Ollie and my mom were so very close, and after Ollie passed, it was like my mom just gave up on life.

No matter what I or my remaining two sisters did, it seemed impossible to reach her. I guess the hardest part was just watching someone we loved drift away, and there seemed to be nothing we could do about it.

I went to church one morning as usual, and I

found myself praying to God to ease my mom's suffering. I know that this was an awful thing to say, but I asked God to take Mom and have her reunited with my dad and sister. That may not have been the right or correct thing to pray for, but to watch her like that, just made me stop and think about finding some way to ease the pain she was in.

I thought about my mom being a head nurse for all those years and couldn't even imagine the support and caring she gave to others. During the sermon, the pastor talked about how important it was to have a life that God would expect of us. I have to say, looking back on the role my mother played in the lives of others, I am speechless given the number of babies she delivered and families she cared for. I left church feeling grateful for the life she'd lived.

Getting told Mom had cancer as well as Alzheimer's was a very hard day. I walked out of her home feeling very lost again as I thought, *What next!* I just wanted her to be comfortable and not suffer; this was my biggest wish. I was so overwhelmed that I called my ex-wife on the phone and asked her to tell my daughter as I could not bring myself to do it. All I can remember was crying so hard that I started to hyperventilate. It felt like I was losing control and could not help or stop this from happening.

As Mom's cancer progressed, it was even harder than dealing with the other health challenges she had. She was so medicated, it was hard just to sit with her. She slept most of the time and would wake up once or twice during my visit, but I knew it would not be long now given her condition. I used to sit and pray for her and just hold her hand, thinking about our entire life together. This was very new to me as I was not around for my father's death, nor was I around for my father-in-law's, so sitting and having the chance to express my thoughts was very hard. But I am glad that I did have the chance to tell her I loved her, and I think she knew it because she squeezed my hand and smiled.

I am just glad that it was not too late for us to reconnect, even if it was this health challenge that brought us back together. I have learned so much from her being with her in this time of need.

Chapter 10
It Is Just Time To Say "Goodbye"

I attended church one morning and prayed for Mom. The pastor was giving his sermon, and he spoke about what it takes to receive the goodness from God.

I have drifted at times in my service to God, but I have always felt deep in my heart that God was involved in my life. Being closer to God made me realize my mom was going to be well looked after in paradise one day.

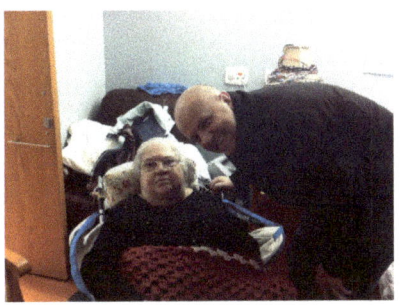

One of the final days that Mom seemed okay but was in and out of awareness. She seemed to be very distant at times, not sure of who I was or even what was happening around her.

When I arrived at the care home later that day, I just had a feeling that it was her time. She had developed pneumonia on top of her cancer, and we decided as a family to stop treatment at that point. The skin cancer spot on her head seemed to be ten times the size that it originally was, and she looked so small in her special wheelchair. I really did not know what to say. I struggled to hold back the tears.

She seemed to be aware of her surroundings, and she actually knew who I was and asked, "Where have you been? I haven't seen you in such a long time." Funny thing was I had been up to visit with her just the week before. I have always wondered why she was on this endless search for me, but maybe it had to do with my early choice in life to separate myself from my family. It's something I ponder a lot to this day.

My sisters and I stayed gathered around her and were all together when she passed. It was the moment we all knew was coming, and there it was. The moment had come. I recalled advice I'd heard about how we always shed tears when our loved ones pass away, but what they really need is love, laughter, and hugs while they're alive. We all looked at each other tearfully in the moment and knew that we had given Mom that.

After her passing, I was sent a note from a close friend with the following poem, and I have never forgotten it.

"The Alzheimer's request"
by Owen Darnell

> Do not ask me to remember,
> Don't try to make me understand,
> Let me rest and know you're with me,
> Kiss my cheek and hold my hand.
> I'm confused beyond your concept,
> I am sad and sick and lost.
> All I know is that I need you
> To be with me at all cost.
> Do not lose your patience with me,
> Do not scold or curse or cry.
> I can't help the way I am acting,
> Can't be different though I try.
> Just remember that I need you,
> That the best of me is gone,
> Please don't fail to stand beside me,
> Love me 'til my life is done.

Never Forgotten

Epilogue
The Reality of Today

It has been several years, three to be exact, since Mom left us. I have unfortunately faced several other challenges myself, being diagnosed with stage three cancer, but by the grace of God, I have been in remission for almost a year now. After getting remarried, my wife Kelly has been my guiding support. I am not sure I would have made it without her and her guidance as a partner in faith, which has helped me see the future so much better.

The experience with my sister's death and my mom's Alzheimer's made me realize the importance of family, and when faced with the challenges that life brings, reconnecting is possible! Reuniting with family, no matter the circumstances: health, death, or distance, is always worth it. Even in the face of Alzheimer's and dementia, do not sit back in silence; take the step to reconnect before it's too late. It's never too late to be there for one another. Apologize, forgive, and create happiness.

Everything you are experiencing at this moment, whatever it is, is exactly what you need for your personal growth. Trust it!

"Have patience, God isn't finished yet."
Philippians 1:6
God bless.

Tribute

I would like to express my gratitude to the staff at Elm for all the care and support you gave my mother throughout this journey.

To my sister Jodi, who was always there for my mom and her "ROCK." As her health challenges came up, you were always there for her and never wavered. The devotion and love you showed her was nothing short of amazing!

To my sister Bev. Thank you for being there for Mom in the supportive and loving way that you did, I know your regular calls to her as well as your visits always lifted her spirits up, and she so looked forward to seeing you.

To my sister Ollie, who passed away almost twelve years ago. I can't recount how many conversations we had at your graveside, with respect to the challenges Mom faced. With that said, I turn her gently over to your care in the presence of God.

About the Author

K. Craig Timlick is a motivational speaker and family group advocate. He has been blessed to share this journey with you and hopes that it inspires you to never give up on the love of family no matter the circumstances.

"Has Anyone Seen My Mom" is the true story of one man's journey to reconnect with his family, particularly his mother, after the death of his sister and through his mother's struggle with Alzheimer's. It's never too late to reconnect with loved ones no matter the circumstances.

www.ingramcontent.com/pod-product-compliance
Lightning Source LLC
Chambersburg PA
CBHW042027050526
44107CB00103B/719